MIDDLE EAST MOVERS

Royal Engineer Transportation

In the Suez Canal Zone 1947 – 1956

by

HUGH MACKINTOSH

Badge of Royal Engineers
Transportation Units under
command Middle East Land Forces

Badge of Royal Engineers
Reserve Army
Transportation Units

ISBN 0948305 10

Published by
North Kent Books
Rochester, Kent.

Printed by
Northfleet Press
5-6 Stonebridge Road, Northfleet, Kent DA11 9BR
Tel: 01474 534484

CONTENTS

SKETCH MAPS

ILLUSTRATIONS

FOREWORD

This slim volume owes its origin to one of those informal groups of old soldiers that reflect the strong and lasting comradeship which is a hallmark of the British soldier. Perhaps through shared endeavour by young men in strange places, far from home, under difficult and often dangerous conditions, seldom understood let alone appreciated for its true worth, soldiering establishes friendships that last a lifetime.

So it was that, on the occasion when an ex War Department locomotive, itself a veteran of the Normandy landings of 1944 but which had reached the end of its working life and was being handed over to the Royal Engineers Museum for safekeeping, a group of old soldiers were grumbling amongst themselves, as old soldiers do, because no-one had written down their story. They were veterans of that part of the Army which, during the 1940s and 1950s, had been the units of the Transportation Service Royal Engineers in the Middle East. Colonel Hugh Mackintosh, himself a distinguished retired Sapper who had just completed Volume XI of the History of the Corps of Royal Engineers, was invited to "volunteer" to write a book. The possibilities were almost endless. Throughout the first half of the twentieth century, railways and docks were fundamental to British operations throughout the Middle East. From Lawrence of Arabia and the Desert Railway, via Allenby, the Desert Campaigns and the capture of Jerusalem 1918, via Auckinleck, Wavell, the carriage of war material to Russia 1941-45 and Montgomery and the Eight Army in 1942 to the Suez Base in 1956, operations hinged on railways, built, maintained and operated by the Royal Engineers.

From such a broad canvas, with contributions and advice from many who were there at the time, not least a splendid Sapper who, in 1999, at the age of 70+ is still rightly proud to describe himself "a shunter at Adabiya", and only too conscious of the sadness of those whose stories would not be included, Hugh knew he could cover only a fraction of the whole. He selected the Canal Zone 1947-54 as his field. As a young officer, he himself had served in the Zone during 1952-55 so knew at first hand the conditions under which railways operated during those troubled times. This book is the result.

Sadly Hugh died suddenly in December 1999, just as his work was starting to progress from manuscript into book. To Hugh for all his efforts, but also to his widow Patricia and the family, our thanks are due for allowing the work to be completed. Hugh hoped that the sale of the book would contribute in a small way to help maintain displays at the Royal Engineers Museum at Chatham.

As the last Commandant of the RE Transportation Centre at Longmoor, to those who served in RE Transportation, in the Middle East or elsewhere, to the many who have no personal experience of the times but for whom railways and history hold an abiding interest – indeed to all who read it - I commend this important record of some of the works and times of British soldiers in Middle East Command.

Major General J.C. Woollett, CBE, MC,
January 2000

INTRODUCTION

Units of the British Army have served in Egypt almost continuously for three quarters of a century, initially to help suppress an internal rebellion and latterly to preserve the integrity of the Suez Canal. In World War One elaborate defences were built along its shores as protection against attack from the Turks, and in World War Two the same area became a huge base for operations in the Western Desert. Since then there have been two occasions when the Army has been deployed in strength to the Canal Zone, once in the early 1950's and again in 1956. Much has been written about the latter, the brief so called Suez Operation, but very little about the previous troubles leading up to it, despite the fact that at its peak over 80,000 troops were deployed in this very restricted, mainly unhealthy, frequently hostile and generally frustrating theatre. Many of those involved were National Servicemen and Reservists who served for months or even years under these conditions without any subsequent recognition. This account is written to record something of the contribution made by those in the Transportation and Movement Control Branches of the Royal Engineers who took part.

The Transportation Branch RE was responsible in war for operating and maintaining the lines of communication of the Army by rail, river and canal, for loading and unloading ships and maintaining all port facilities above the high water mark. In the 1939-1945 War there were 146,000 officers and men in the Branch world wide, and among their notable achievements was the building and operation of Mulberry Harbour at Arromanches.

Until recently, a Headquarters Staff Branch known as Q (Movements) was responsible for arranging priorities and rates of flow for all personnel, vehicles, stores and equipment. Their instructions were passed down through men of the Movement Control Branch working in ports, railway stations, airports and elsewhere on the lines of communication.

CHAPTER ONE

BACKGROUND

Historical

The aftermath of World War Two left a large number of British troops in Iraq, Syria, Palestine and Egypt, together with a comprehensive network of railways, ports, docks and workshops. Even before the war was over, and despite their presence in Egypt being covered by the Anglo Egyptian Treaty of 1936, discussions about the eventual withdrawal of all British troops from that country had taken place. In 1945, spurred on by extremist attacks on British clubs and property in Cairo and Alexandria, the establishment of a Middle East Base in Palestine was actively being pursued. Another project being conducted was the construction of a huge Stores Holding Depot at Mackinnon Road in Kenya, but this was soon to be aborted because considerable delays, frustrations, labour and transport problems made it no longer viable.

Meanwhile all was not well in Palestine. Pressure for the setting up of a Jewish state in what was at the time a predominantly Arab country was encouraged by ever increasing terrorist attacks against British targets. In November 1947 the United Nations decreed that the land should be partitioned, and it was announced in the House of Commons that the evacuation of British Forces would be completed by August 1948.

By this time the Russian threat to the Middle East oilfields had strengthened the case for Britain to maintain in the long term a firm base somewhere in the area. Additionally there was always the need to protect the Suez Canal as a vital artery for trade between Europe and the Far East. As there still remained some £100m worth of weapons, ammunition, vehicles and equipment stored in Egypt from the end of the war, and the 1936 Anglo-Egyptian Treaty still had another eight years to run, Egypt was clearly the preferred option as the location for the long term Middle East Base.

The 1936 Treaty allowed for full occupation of the country in the event of war, but in peace only permitted the stationing of troops and installations along the shores of the Canal. Under its terms, accommodation for 10,000 troops and 400 RAF Personnel were to have been provided by the Egyptian authorities inside the Zone. The original plan had been to enlarge the existing depots at Tel el Kebir (TEK) and Moascar on the outskirts of Ismailia, and to build a new cantonment at Fayid on the shores of the Great Bitter Lake for General Headquarters Middle East Land Forces. But few buildings had been constructed by the end of the War, so when in 1947 and 1948 the British Army dutifully withdrew from the delights of the capital city and elsewhere, and concentrated instead on the sandy wastes alongside the Canal, many of them were forced to live under canvas, within the area defined by the Treaty.

The Canal Zone

The map attached to the 1936 Treaty defined the western boundary of the Canal Zone as a line running from Kantara to a point ten kilometres west of Tel el Kebir, then south west down the Ismailia Canal to the 31 deg 30 min easting, due south to the Iron Tower in the Mashkara Hills, south east to the 29 deg 30 min northing at Sheikh el Winag in the Gebel Bahariya hills, and then due east to emerge in the Gulf of Suez at a point some ten kilometres south of Ain Sukhna. Curiously, the eastern boundary was not defined but always assumed to be the bank of the Suez Canal. Throughout the Zone there were good roads built to service the Canal. In addition roads were constructed under the Treaty – known as Treaty roads - to which military vehicles were officially confined. There were also primitive vehicle ferries across the canals at various points.

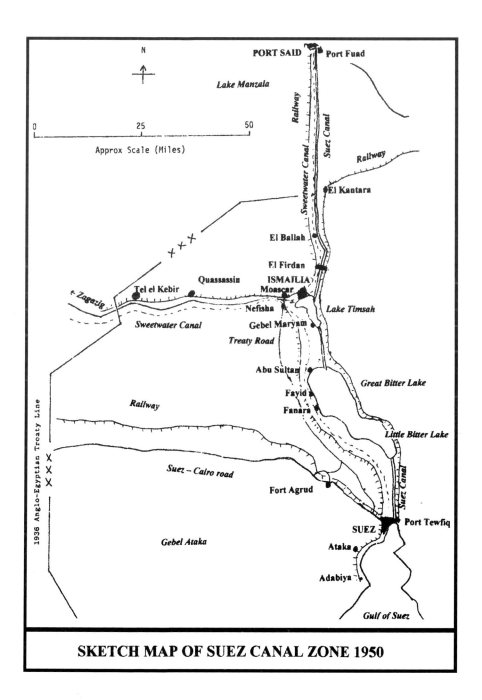

SKETCH MAP OF SUEZ CANAL ZONE 1950

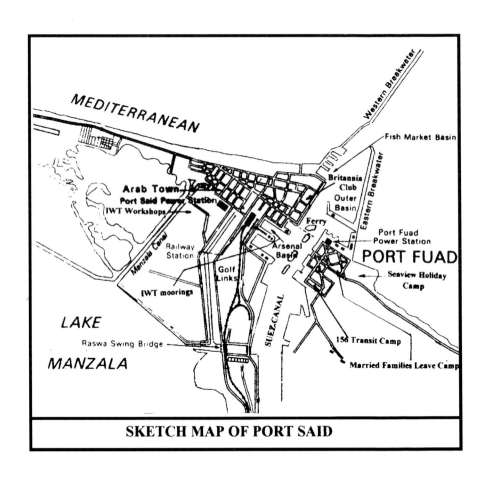

SKETCH MAP OF PORT SAID

12

Until the 1914-1918 war the only railway into the area was a single track standard gauge from Cairo to Ismailia. A second track alongside was then built by the Egyptian State Railways in 1915. A single line had also been built on the west bank of the Canal from Port Said to Suez, which was doubled as far as Kantara in 1916. At the same time, using two railway companies from France, the Royal Engineers built a mixed gauge light railway on the eastern side of the Canal. Most of these expansions were brought about by the need to support the Desert Campaign of 1916-1917 against the Turkish Army in Palestine.

By the end of World War Two there was therefore a well established rail network linking the major towns and operated by the Egyptian State Railways. A single line now also ran from Cairo to Suez, and the line up the east bank of the Canal had been improved from Suez to Kantara where it joined the Palestine Railway. The only rail crossing of the Canal was at El Firdan where a 300 metre long swing bridge had been built in 1941 to replace two fixed ferries powered by steam winches. There were rail marshalling yards which had been built in 1940 at Suez and Nefisha, and a military rail spur from Suez to the docks at Adabiya. The main civilian ports were at Port Said and Suez.

When de Lesseps built the Canal he also constructed a channel from the River Nile to supply the work force with water, known as the Sweetwater Canal. This name could hardly have been more inappropriate because by the time with which we are concerned it was in use by the locals for everything including waste and sewage disposal. As a result, and despite being the only source of fresh water for the troops in the Zone, it was a considerable health hazard, exacerbated by the heat and flies and generally low standard of local hygiene.

Topography

Looking in more detail at the map and starting in the north, Port Said was a large town, dominated by the port facilities at the entrance to the Canal, and unable to expand because it was hemmed in by the

Mediterranean on one side and Lake Mansala on the other. Standing prominently at the entrance to the harbour stood a huge thirty four foot high pedestal, surmounted by a twenty two foot statue of Ferdinand de Lesseps, creator of the Canal, erected by the French in 1899 only to be blown up by the Egyptians in 1956.

In the early post war years the port was familiar to many on board the troopships heading to and from the Far East for its amalgam of smells, gulli-gulli men, dirty postcards, and chicos calling "You come and see my sister, velly cheap!" In fact its reputation was such that the Services Guide gave strict instructions to soldiers stationed or on leave there. Extracts included:

"Arab Town is Out of Bounds; if you do enter it you will be beaten up and robbed."
"Gulli-gulli men may be clever; don't lend them any money for a trick however because although they know how to make it disappear they have not yet learnt how to bring it back."
"All brothels are Out of Bounds. They are filthy dirty, in a filthy area and full of horrible diseases."

There were, however, cafes and bars which could be used and a number of clubs including the NAAFI Britannia Club for Other Ranks, the Sea View holiday camp and married families leave camp at Port Fuad opposite the town. As most troop movements at the time were still done by sea, there was a large 156 Transit Camp for servicemen entering and leaving the area, and several well known large stores such as Simon Artz.

For the first few miles south of Port Said, the Canal passed through the salt marshes of Lake Manzala until Kantara. Here the Palestine Railway ran alongside the east bank having come across the Sinai. Between Kantara and the swing bridge at El Firdan a second canal, called the Farouk Bypass, was opened in 1948. This provided an alternative on the western side for shipping using the Suez Canal.

SERVICES GUIDE

TO

PORT SAID

CANAL COMPANY BUILDING

SECURITY

The contents of this Guide must not be communicated to the Press. It is for the information of Services personnel only

PUBLISHED BY A.W.S. CANAL NORTH DISTRICT

Price P.T. 1

Married Families Leave Camp — Port Fouad

Run by N.A.A.F.I./E.F.I. For all service Officers and other ranks, married families, with excellent facilities for the care of children of all ages.

Cocktail Bars, lounges, shops, hairdressing and laundry services, kiddies' play rooms, ornamental pool and a children's nurse in attendance if required.

Excellent food, well served, either indoors or outdoors, under gaily-coloured awnings.

Dancing and bathing available.

For further information apply to :—

Resident Supervisor,
Married Families,
Holiday Camp,
PORT FOUAD.

Seaview Holiday Camp - Port Fouad

For ORs of All Services, including all women's services. Delightfully situated in Port Fouad with amenities to suit every taste and excellent accommodation for 700 Guests. Spacious dining room, lounges, reading rooms, quiet room and writing rooms, music room, ladies and gents hairdressing shop, book - shops, gift shop, and a wide range of books to choose from in the library.

The Club House contains one of the finest billiard rooms n he Middle East also a table tennis and darts room and there six very excellent hard tennis courts, icket pitch, football nets, and tennis-quoit nets. Equipt is available at all times for every form of outdoor t and there are facilities for horse riding in the ip and there is a cycle hire store.

The Open Air Cinema has a change of programme times a week and shows the latest films from Eng-. The Cinema is also used to present other shows n these are available in the area.

For those of you who enjoy dancing, the open air dance r at Seaview offers excellent dancing four times a k to the music of an eight piece orchestra. On Sa-ay night a Grand Carnival Dance and Cabaret Show eld till midnight.

The beach is only a few minutes walk from any part iea View Holiday Camp and after an evenings en-ainment on the dance floor what could be better i a moonlight swim before turning in,?

The Britannia Club

For W.O's, Sergts and O.R's only

This is surely the most luxurious club in the Middle East. On the premises there are a first class Cinema, a NAAFI Gift shop, an excellent restaurant, a Buffet bar, a billiard room, a music room, reading and writing rooms, a barbers shop etc. Indoor games of many variety are available free of charge. The Club is excellently and tastefully furnished throughout and the mural paintings of British scenes and country life, are well worth seeing. Dances are given three times weekly under the supervision of the W.V.S.

The Club is run by NAAFI/EFI and the prices charged for food and liquor are much below those charged in civil establishments. It is also well to remember that the Club is under Military supervision for hygiene and sanitation.

---

1. Excerpts from the Services Guide to what was available in Port Said, issued about the end of World War Two.

(L J D Ball)

15

2. New Garden AKC
   cinema, Port Said.
   (D B Hickman)

3. Ferdinand de Lesseps statue at the
   entrance to Port Said (unveiled in
   1899, blown up in 1956).
   (D B Hickman)

4. Entrance to Sea View
   holiday camp, Port
   Fuad.
   (D B Hickman)

16

5. RE tug off Port Said.
   (*D B Hickman*)

6. IWT floating dock
   at Port Said.
   (*D B Hickman*)

7. IWT launch at
   Port Said.
   (*D B Hickman*)

8. Ex United States diesel locos used by 10 Rly Sqn.
(M Rhodes, H Begg)

9. Typical VC loco nameplate.
(M Rhodes, H Begg)

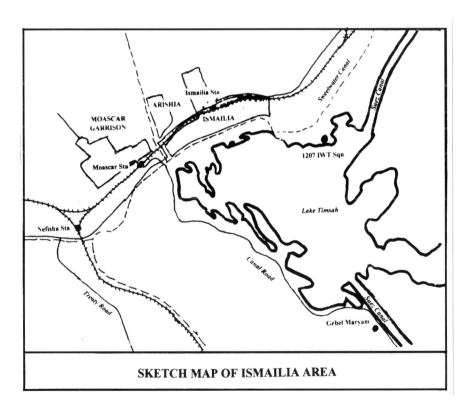

SKETCH MAP OF ISMAILIA AREA

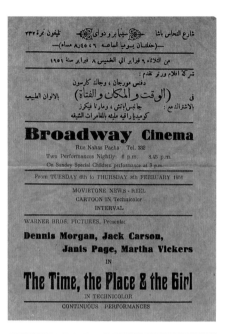

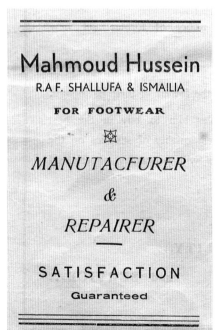

10. Memorabilia. (*G V Cox, P Wells*)

20

On the shores of Lake Timsah lay the green and sophisticated town of Ismailia, headquarters of the Suez Canal Company, with many of its roads and public buildings named in French as a result. Alongside lay the pre-war garrison of Moascar, holding the Headquarters of British Troops, Egypt. Here were well watered, well laid out barracks, including such niceties as a hospital, stadium, schools, clubs and even a very typical English Anglican church. Nearby was a major RAF station, and Headquarters Middle East Air Force.

To the west on the road from Ismailia to Cairo lay Quassassin, storage area for stocks of Royal Engineer construction plant, and Tel el Kebir, the main Middle East reserves storage depot. This huge Base Installation was alleged to hold within its six mile perimeter fence enough stores and vehicles to equip at least four divisions should the need arise.

At the southern end of Lake Timsah lay Gebel Maryam, site during World War Two of the Middle East School of Military Engineering, and a bridging camp. On the summit of the Gebel stood the twin obelisks of the War Memorial commemorating the Allied defence of the Canal in the World War One. At Abu Sultan, where the Canal entered the Great Bitter Lake, there was a Base Ammunition Depot from where old and unsafe ordnance was loaded onto Z craft for dumping at sea.

The Great Bitter Lake, unlike its Little neighbour, was deep enough to accommodate shipping and was some ten miles long by five miles wide. Along the western shore or inland nearby lay an array of mainly military installations including Fayid, Fanara, Kasfareet, Geneifa, Shallufa and Kabrit.

Some semi-permanent accommodation had been built at Fayid by April 1947, mostly of Nissen and other huts, to provide offices, married quarters, a hospital, a 5 Megawatt power station, messes, clubs, welfare facilities, and offices for GHQ MELF. Much of this construction work had been done under Operation SATIRE (the move out of Cairo and Alexandria) which employed German and Italian prisoners of war under

RE supervision. There was also an adjacent RAF airfield that served as the main entry point into the Zone for air transport and air trooping aircraft. In those days unit trooping was almost entirely carried out by sea, while individuals often went overland to and from the Middle East by train and boat via the "Medloc" route. This method of travel was however gradually being replaced by using shatteringly noisy York and slightly quieter Hermes charter aircraft. For these journeys troops assembled in London at Goodge Street deep shelters, which had been turned into a Movement Control Assembly Centre, before flying out from Blackbushe to Fayid via Malta.

The dock facilities for Fayid were at Fanara a mile further south, which was itself a stores holding area, served by road, rail and an oil pipeline, with an adjacent oil jetty and fuel installations including a jerrycan factory. It had also been a flying boat station, originally for the Imperial Airways and latterly for the RAF.

At the southernmost end of the Canal lay Suez, an old town considerably expanded when the new waterway was built. Opposite the town lay Port Tewfiq, built on an artificial peninsula using the earth excavated when the canal was dug. An oil refinery with associated storage tanks was adjacent to Suez while the main dock area was at Port Tewfiq with the entrance to the Canal beyond.

Some ten miles further south on the banks of the Gulf of Suez lay the military port of Adabiya (pronounced "'ad a beer?"). There, docks had been built in 1942 as a major project under RE supervision, to provide a deep water port for the Services. It included a quay one thousand feet long to which ships of up to twenty six foot draught could be brought alongside. It was served by its own steam cranes, storage sheds and rail spur, so that military cargoes could be handled independently of the shipping using Suez and the Canal.

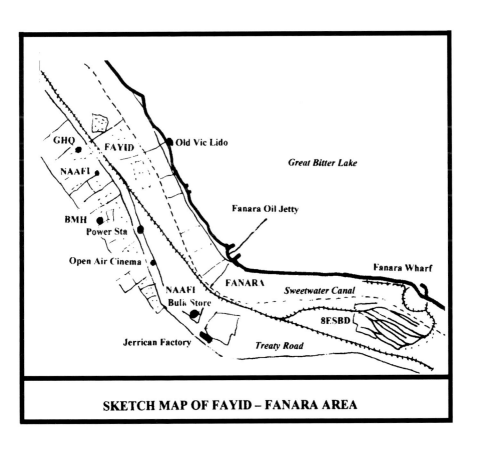

GHQ
FAYID
Old Vic Lido
NAAFI
Great Bitter Lake
BMH
Power Sta
Fanara Oil Jetty
Open Air Cinema
Fanara Wharf
NAAFI
Bulk Store
FANARA
Sweetwater Canal
8ESBD
Jerrican Factory
Treaty Road

SKETCH MAP OF FAYID – FANARA AREA

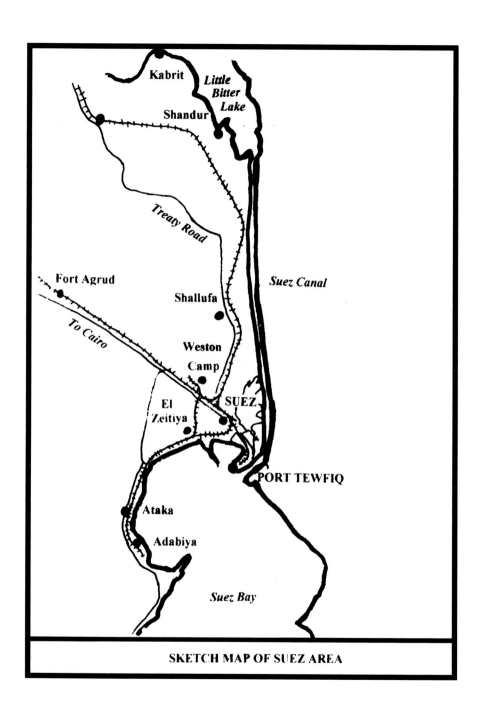

Kabrit

Little Bitter Lake

Shandur

Treaty Road

Fort Agrud

Suez Canal

Shallufa

To Cairo

Weston Camp

El Zeitiya

SUEZ

PORT TEWFIQ

Ataka

Adabiya

Suez Bay

SKETCH MAP OF SUEZ AREA

Palestine

Meanwhile in Palestine the original Hejaz Railway, built by the Turks early in the century and used to carry pilgrims to Medina had been enlarged. By now it included a line from Egypt across the Sinai, originally built to support Allenby in World War One, and which had been further extended in World War Two. By the time of the ending of the British Mandate in 1947 much of the responsibility for construction, maintenance and operation of the railways was in the hands of the Royal Engineers. In particular this was carried out by 193 Railway Operating Squadron and 603 Railway Construction Squadron, supported by 199 Railway Workshops. After the announcement of the withdrawal and despite repeated terrorist attacks and sabotage these units managed to recover some 270,000 tons of equipment which was then transported overland to Egypt, or by sea elsewhere from Haifa. For this task the docks were operated by 1261 Port Operating and 1207 Inland Water Transport Squadrons, the civilian labour having largely defected.

General living conditions in The Zone

In the areas around Ismailia the daytime temperatures often rose to 36 degrees C in summer, but nights could be cool, though never dropping below eight degrees even in winter. Further south and particularly in the hills and deserts summer temperatures could soar to nearly 40 degrees. Between March and May a burning southerly wind, the Khamsin, often blew, carrying blinding sand into the eyes. It seldom rained in the Zone except lightly in winter.

Apart from the naturally growing palms, the remaining bushes and trees, such as acacia, jacaranda, eucalyptus, tamarisk and mimosa visible in such places as Ismailia, were almost entirely ornamental, and dependent on artificial irrigation for survival. There was a complete absence of locally grown green vegetables and fruit, which resulted in huge stocks of these items having to be imported from elsewhere in the Mediterranean to supply all the armed services and their families.

Until the emergency arose in 1951, basic conditions were generally bearable for the troops stationed in the area. Morale however was not high because of the presence of wartime soldiers frustrated at delays in their demobilisation and the antipathy of most of the local population. The latter were traditionally despised by the British soldier. Even the stars on their national flag were rudely referred to as "Maleesh, Mafish and Baksheesh" as if they represented the main native preoccupations.

Hours of work were generally confined to mornings in the summer with an early start, with transport often provided for swimming and evening activities. Bars and clubs were set up by NAAFI, YMCA and Toc H, and sport was encouraged, though playing association and rugby football or hockey on rolled dirt pitches incurred frequent injuries and skin infections. AKC cinemas were usually open-air which, to quote Soldier magazine at the time:

"If you don't mind birds flying overhead can be very pleasant. Downwind, you can hear Bob Hope wisecracking from 100 yards away, all for nothing."

Many units put on camp concerts and their own revues, particularly in the winter months. Sapper Geoff Cox of 10 Railway Squadron, who in addition to his railway duties trained as a bugler and cinema projectionist, recalls entertaining troops throughout the Zone. In addition touring companies such as the Ivy Benson Girls Band and ENSA occasionally came out from the UK to entertain the troops.

Some shops in the towns were In Bounds, and within the camps small local traders set up stalls, often with over-inflated names such as Harrods, Marks and Spencer, and Burtons. Most purchases could be made at NAAFI and YMCA sports shops, but soldiers had little money to spare – a Regular sapper's basic pay was between sixty and ninety shillings a week. This did not go far on a basic diet of Stella or Keo beer and a few cheap cigarettes – a tin of fifty Players cost one and ninepence. Incidentally, we have to remember that smoking was not frowned upon in those days; in fact in some ways it was actively encouraged.

Probably the major hazard for everyone in this part of the world was pilfering. The local Egyptians were masters in the art, and went to extraordinary lengths of ingenuity or just plain cheek to achieve success. Vehicles were jacked up and their wheels removed overnight under the eyes of guards, and stores – even those assumed to be most unattractive – mysteriously disappeared. Phil Wells of 10 Squadron remembers that between Fanara wharf and Fayid there were sharp curves on the railway line, hidden by palms. Stores such as corrugated iron sheets were discharged from the IWT coaster Peter Lee onto tank flats for transit. Many of these would have vanished by the time the flats reached 8 Engineer Stores Base Depot in Fayid, despite the supposedly watchful eyes of the Mauritian guards riding shotgun on the train. On another occasion an enterprising employee removed a complete blacksmith's anvil by suspending it on a chain round his neck, concealed beneath his galabiya.

CHAPTER TWO

THE EARLY POST WAR YEARS

By September 1947 the Transportation units in Egypt had been grouped together as 4 Port Operating Group, consisting of six squadrons responsible between them for all military rail and port operations within the theatre, including the use of lighterage craft. By 1949 however, with the general run down of forces in the area, this Group had been disbanded and the units reduced to 10 Railway Squadron, 169 Railway Workshops Squadron, 53 Port Squadron and 1207 Inland Water Transport Squadron and Workshops. These were all under the command of Middle East Transportation Regiment, with its Headquarters at Fayid.

10 Rly Sqn

One of the only two Regular Transportation units in existence at the outbreak of World War Two, 10 Squadron ended the war in Klagenfurt in Austria, engaged in railway repairs. In 1947 the unit moved to Egypt to Adabiya camp, later to be known as Elphinstone camp, with a strength of six officers and 250 Other Ranks. Thereafter it was primarily employed in the handling of military freight trains on the Egyptian State Railway system within the Canal Zone, and was wholly responsible for the running of the military branch line from Suez to Adabiya Docks. For this purpose much of the rolling stock was held at the sidings of the Transportation Storage Depot outside Suez adjacent to 169 Railway Workshops. There was a small locomotive depot at Checkers, Adabiya, and the Squadron also ran the Derby Diesel locos used to assemble stores trains within TEK garrison.

In 1948 a detachment was sent to reopen and run the Western Desert railway between Benghazi, Barce and Sollum and the Squadron also had detachments within the Zone at Moascar and Fanara. It was at the latter, at Peking camp, that one of the more unusual events took place.

(*D Waller*)

11. 10 Railway Squadron 1950.

12. Locomotive inspection shed at Fanara.
(*W Warren*)

13. Interior of shed used
as a hanging pit.
(*W Warren*)

The death penalty for murder was still in force in 1950 and Corporal Warren recalls a hanging taking place in the camp:

"One day the Military Police told us to leave our compound and move tents into the desert because they wanted to use our offices as cells and the loco shed as a hanging pit. Two British and three Mauritian soldiers were I believe then hung for murder".

169 Rly Wksp Sqn

169 Railway Workshops had been formed from the wartime 1169 unit of that name, and had been located at Weston camp about six miles outside the centre of Suez since 1941. At this time, it employed only thirty RE rank and file and a large number of civilians, including German prisoners of war and a few ex-RAF personnel awaiting demob. The unit was joined in 1947 by 199 Workshops from Jaffa when that unit with the rest of the army withdrew from Palestine.

During that withdrawal much use was made by rail traffic of the swing bridge at El Firdan to transfer troops from Palestine into Egypt. It was particularly unfortunate therefore that at the height of this operation, on 16th November 1947, a Dutch ship chose to hit the bridge, depositing one half of it in the Canal and thereby effectively severing the only direct rail link. However, fortunately there were still the two ancient cable operated ferries alongside which had been out of action for some time, but which when in working order could carry just four wagons at a time. Lieut Currie of 169 was therefore sent as a matter of urgency with a section from his Workshops to re-commission the steam boilers and winches by which the ferries were operated, in order that troop movement could continue without undue delay.

Although the war had by now been over for a few years, control of stores was still inclined to be a little haphazard as peace time accounting had not yet been fully implemented. Capt Ross Mason recalls an occasion when he was called to check the equipment of 169 at Adabiya and the conversation went something like this:

"Let us start with the two breakdown cranes on charge."
"Two, Sir? We only have one in the yard."
(A quick check outside revealed one complete crane and one jib.)
"Ah well, Sir. You see, one crane was in steam but was banked down for the night. However somehow it got up steam by itself and moved off onto the ESR track and ran down the slope to Port Tewfiq through the buffers and into the water. That must be its jib, Sir."

53 Port Sqn

Also living at Weston camp was the Headquarters and Adabiya Troop of 53 Port Squadron, responsible for the operation of Adabiya Docks. The unit was mainly made up of stevedores, checkers, fitters, crane and vehicle drivers, and included RAF personnel to handle their own specialist stores. The Squadron also had some responsibility for the Royal Navy boom defences used in war to protect the southern end of the Canal. Sapper Michael Henry, who was a National Service crane operator and fitter in the unit, tells how:

"We used to parade at 0530 hrs, go by truck the 20 miles to the docks, and return at about 1330 hrs. Under a lance corporal and with one other sapper we had a gang of eight Egyptians, repairing and maintaining all types of cranes."

There was a troop at Fanara and another in Aqaba in what was then Transjordan. No 1 Troop at Fanara was in a small camp on the waterfront with its own NAAFI and an RAF cinema only a hundred yards away. The Troop was joined each day by local working parties who transferred stores from ship to barge, barge to quay, and by crane to road or rail transport. Sapper Blake recalls that at times, as the camp was so close to the quay, if accidents occurred or hazardous cargo was being handled, their tents would have to be temporarily abandoned. And on one occasion there was a fight among the crew of a ship diverted from Abadan and a party from the Squadron were sent aboard to restore order.

The Troop at Aqaba consisted of two officers, a few Senior NCO's and about 20 Sappers. Aqaba was a shallow port, though crude efforts were made to deepen it by using a dragline standing on a Z craft. Ships usually anchored offshore, and the detachment used the ships' derricks to unload over the side onto Z craft. These craft were then unloaded using the crawler cranes on the dockside. Much of the cargo was heading for British Army units still in Jordan and the RAF in Habbaniya and Mafraq in Iraq.

1207 IWT Sqn

1207 Inland Water Transport Squadron had their headquarters at Ismailia in a tented camp on the shores of Lake Timsah. They were responsible for crewing all inland waterway craft including tugs, lighters and the Z craft already mentioned. These latter were a special form of shallow draught landing craft, with a flat deck 70 feet long, capable of carrying up to 200 tons, with a crew of a sergeant, corporal and four sappers. They had originally been designed for the carriage of personnel and troops along the North African coast in World War Two, and were built in India and assembled on Chevalier Island on the north of Lake Timsah. One of the many operations in which they took part was the carriage of troops and stores across the Canal at Ferry Point outside Ismailia during the evacuation from Palestine. The Squadron had detachments in Alexandria, Tobruk, Port Said, Suez and Famagusta in Cyprus. There was also an IWT Workshops at Port Said which served all units in the theatre.

There was some excitement for many of the troops in the northern half of the Zone in 1948. In May of that year the First Arab-Israeli war broke out, when troops from Egypt, Syria and Jordan attacked the Jews in the newly forming state of Israel. Having suffered previously from the ignominy of being jeered at by the Egyptians as they left Cairo and moved into the Zone, the same troops could now enjoy watching the bedraggled remnants of a defeated Egyptian army streaming home to Cairo.

Later there was to be much activity in 10 Squadron. By 1950 the main line locos from elsewhere in the theatre had started being delivered into Adabiya. In July the Egyptian authorities allowed them to be used within the Canal Zone, albeit with ESR pilots. On occasion they even allowed them to work to and from Cairo for wheel balancing. The 10 Squadron crews working over the main line network were constantly switched to enable the maximum number to learn the routes, and this was to prove a great help later during the emergency.

The majority of these locos were the famous Stanier 8F 2-8-0 freight engines, originally designed in the nineteen thirties for the LMS railway. Early in the War the Ministry of Transport decreed that, because of their proven reliability and performance, production should be concentrated on this design for main freight haulage. By the end of 1945 some 650 had been built, and many oil fired versions were serving overseas in the Middle and Near East.

Within the Canal Zone, in recognition that these locos were being operated by the Royal Engineers, a number of them were named after RE officers and men who had been awarded the Victoria Cross in the Crimean War. These are listed at Annex A in this publication. Typical was the naming of loco 70387 as "Cpl WJ Lendrim VC" on Tuesday 23rd January 1951 by the Engineer in Chief, Major General AD Campbell. The engine had been "bulled up" by being painted black with narrow maroon bands round the boiler. The wheel rims and buffers were painted white, and the crank rods and running gear highly polished.

The Squadron Commander of 10 Squadron at this time was a certain Major GCL Alexander. On the arrival of a Sapper General, Sir Brian Robertson, as Commander in Chief MELF in 1950, Major Alexander claimed the right of his Squadron to provide the Guard of Honour as 10

14. Married families boarding the engine "Lt W O Lennox VC" after the naming ceremony on 6 May 1950 by the Chief Engineer MELF, Maj Gen Broomhall CB DSO OBE.

(G V Cox)

15. Weston camp outside Suez.
(A Trout)

16. The ever present threat of sleepers, fishplates and whole rails being stolen overnight. (*D Waller*)

17. Locomotive "Cpl Lendrim VC" with Spr Wells. (*P Wells*)

18. Maintenance gang at Adabiya 1950 *(M. Henry)*

19. SS "Eastern Med" on fire at Adabiya Docks on 22 Nov 50. Note the Royal Navy boom defence equipment in the foreground, (left) and surplus empty jerricans marking out the tent lines (below).
(W. Warren)

20. (below) All that remained of the burnt out ship the following morning.
(W. Warren)

21. Checkers loco depot 1951.

(M Rhodes)

22. Adabiya (later named Elphinstone) camp 1951.

(D. Waller)

Squadron was the senior RE unit in the theatre. Thereafter he instituted his own guard mounting ceremony at the Squadron camp, despite the fact that it was miles from any public eye. The ceremony was accompanied by appropriate calls on the bugle and handover of keys and included the orders:

"Old guard to the new guard, present arms!
New guard to the old guard, present arms!"

On the 22nd November 1950 there was a major fire at Adabiya docks. On the morning of that Wednesday an ex-Canadian Lakes Greek owned steamer, the SS Eastern Med, was discharging a deck cargo of jerricans filled with fuel. The cans had unwisely been stacked on top of the hot steam pipes which operated the winches. While the unloading was in process, one of the cans was dropped, an explosion followed, and fire broke out immediately. With black smoke pouring from the ship, the Egyptian dock workers fled. They were only stopped by the sentry on the gate firing a shot, so that a roll call could be taken to see who was missing. Warrant Officer Phillips, in charge of the Adabiya troop of 53 Squadron, and who was subsequently awarded the MBE for gallantry, boarded the ship and attempted to put out the fire. However the inferno was soon too great and by now, being unable to regain the shore, he was rescued from the seaward side by Sapper Davis drawing alongside in a boat. Meanwhile a party assembled by Warrant Officer Harris managed to move the unit dockside cranes and railway wagons away from the immediate vicinity of the burning ship, which remained on fire for the remainder of that day and on into the night. Spilt fuel on the water surface was also ablaze and eventually the ship sank until only her superstructure was visible, by which time it was clear that several members of the native crew had been lost.

Throughout this period the staff within the Movements Branches at Fayid and Moascar were busy with their largely unrewarding work in scheduling the movement of personnel and stores between road, rail and sea transport. This involved the issuing of Movement Orders to all concerned and the provision of staff including RTOs at key points, such as Port Said, Moascar, Fayid and Suez, to assist in their implementation. They were also responsible for the Military Forwarding Organisation which handled troops' unaccompanied personal heavy baggage, and even, from time to time, for the provision of security couriers. They provided an Embarkation Staff Officer who went out by launch to meet every troopship at sea before it entered the Canal, irrespective of the time of day. This could be hazardous in rough weather, as often only rope ladders were available for boarding the ships. Normally all Movements staff were RE, though Frank Sutton, a young officer on the Q (Mov) Staff of GHQ, was surprised to find his relief was a Captain in the RTR. Apparently a clerk somewhere had misinterpreted his award for gallantry as a posting to Movement Control!

23. Officers' Mess Adabiya.

(D Waller)

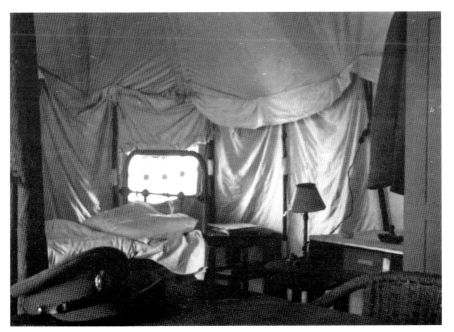
24. Officer's tent interior.

(D Waller)

THE DAILY TELEGRAPH AND MORNING POST, November 19, 1951.

The Dai

No. 30,072   LONDON, MONDAY, NOVEMBER 19, 1951

GUERRILLA WAR IN CANAL ZONE TOWN

5 BRITONS, 9 EGYPTIANS REPORTED KILLED

TROOPS FIRED ON BY ISMAILIA POLICE

WOMEN & CHILDREN MOVED INTO SAFETY AREAS

Clashes between British troops and Egyptian police have taken place in the Suez Canal Zone town of Ismailia. They started on Saturday night and continued yesterday.

According to Egyptian sources five Britons and nine Egyptians were killed. The British figures relate only to Saturday, when a major was found dead after police opened fire on a patrol of the Royal Lincolnshire Regiment.

Colin Reid, special correspondent of THE DAILY TELEGRAPH in the Canal Zone, cabling last night, said that a state of guerrilla warfare existed in Ismailia. A tour of the town indicated that the Egyptian police had relinquished control.

British families were evacuated from their homes to the safety of Service compounds. Families not yet evacuated were guarded by patrols, who were under fire from shuttered windows.

PATROLS GUARD FAMILIES

From COLIN REID,
Daily Telegraph Special Correspondent
ISMAILIA, Sunday.

The situation in Ismailia to-night developed into guerrilla warfare. Under order of the Cairo Government, Egyptian police here were firing practically at sight on British Army vehicles.

So far the British authorities have reported the following casualties over the week-end. One major killed, two other officers seriously wounded, and an unknown number of other ranks

"AGGRESSION" CHARGE BY EGYPTIANS

The Da

No. 30,089   LONDON, SATURDAY, DECEMBER 8, 1951

PARATROOPS MOVE TO SUEZ

ACTION TO PROTECT WATER SUPPLY TO-DAY

CAIRO ORDERS POLICE TO RESIST

BRITISH ENVOY WARNED OF "SERIOUS CONSEQUENCES"

The 16th Parachute Brigade, it was reported from the Canal Zone yesterday, has been moved to Suez to cover the construction of a new safe road from the garrison to the water purification plant outside the port. Terrorist bomb-throwing has almost put the plant out of action.

Lt.-Gen. Sir George Erskine, commanding British troops in Egypt, said yesterday that the operation would begin at dawn to-day. It would involve the bull-dozing of "several Egyptian mud huts."

Egyptian police have received instructions from Cairo to resist the British operations if they are carried out by force. This was announced by Serag el-Din Pasha, Minister of the Interior, after an emergency Cabinet meeting.

Serag el-Din Pasha said he had warned Sir Ralph Stevenson, British Ambassador, of the "serious consequences" of the projected operation. Sir Ralph, he said, had telephoned Gen. Erskine and asked him to try to reconsider the situation, but the general had replied that he would go ahead with his plans for the security of his forces.

WARNING BY BRITISH G.O.C.

From COLIN REID,
Daily Telegraph Special Correspondent
FAYID, Friday.

At dawn to-morrow British troops will demolish huts and hovels on the fringe of Suez to begin a new road from

25a. Daily Telegraph front pages late 1951.

42

Daily Tel

No 30,129 LONDON, S₂ &nd **Morning Post**

BRITISH CAPTURE POLICE H.Q.

46 EGYPTIANS KILLED IN ISMAILIA CLASH

800 DISARMED: TANKS BACK OPERATION

SHIPS MOVE FROM MALTA: CAIRO "EMERGENCY"

British troops yesterday disarmed 800 Egyptian police in Ismailia. Centurion tanks and infantry attacked and captured the police H.Q. after a call to give up their arms had been rejected by the Egyptians.

Four British soldiers were killed and nine wounded. According to the Egyptian Ministry of the Interior 46 Egyptians were killed and 72 wounded. These casualties were inflicted by retaliatory fire after the police had received a "no surrender" order from Cairo.

A state of emergency was declared in Cairo and Alexandria last night after thousands of demonstrators called for revenge on the British. An emergency Cabinet meeting was called by Nahas Pasha, the Prime Minister. It met for four hours and will meet again to-morrow.

Ten British warships left Malta yesterday. It was reported last night that they were steaming eastward to take up emergency dispositions as ordered by Adml. Sir John Edelsten, C.-in-C. Mediterranean Station. An Admiralty statement said that "the C.-in-C. may consider that some reinforcement in the Canal Zone may be necessary."

"NO SURRENDER" ORDER FROM CAIRO

From COLIN REID,
Daily Telegraph Special Correspondent
ISMAILIA, Friday.

British troops to-day disarmed Ismailia's 500 armed polic after they had been dislodged from

MAP shows area of clash between British troops and Egyptian police at Ismailia.

10 WARSHIPS LEAVE, MAY BE BOUND FOR CANAL

By NOWELL HALL,
Daily Telegraph Naval Correspondent

Ten warships, including two cruisers, the light fleet carrier Ocean, a fast minelayer and destroyers, left Malta unexpectedly yesterday. Last night they were reported to be steering eastward to take up emergency dispositions as ordered by Adml. Sir John Edelsten, C.-in-C. Mediterranean.

The Admiralty could not confirm any such movements, pointing out that such decisions are, in the first place, usually left to "the man on the spot." But a hint of the destination of some of the units at sea is contained in the following guarded official statement issued last night:

"Information received in the Admiralty indicates that the Commander-in-Chief Mediterranean (Adml. Sir John H. Edelsten, K.C.B., C.B.E.), has, or is, calling a number of his ships from Malta.

The Admiralty is not in a position to comment beyond observing that the Commander-in-Chief may

FIREMEN WANT NEW TRIBUNAL

16s 6d PAY AWARD "AN INSULT"

DAILY TELEGRAPH REPORTER
A resolution calling on the Ministry of Labour to appoint

ISMAILIA

1. The weekend has seen grave disturbances in ISMAILIA as a direct result of panic and loss of control on the part of the Egyptian Police.

On Saturday evening a patrol of 1 R.LINCOLNS proceeding towards French Square discovered an Egyptian policeman asleep on the pavement. He fled in hysterical panic, firing his rifle. The firing was taken up by other police from a police post nearby and the British patrol took local cover. The Egyptian police continued to fire at the patrol who were forced to return the fire before withdrawing to their base at Army Mansions. During this exchange three Egyptian policemen were wounded and the British patrol suffered no casualties. It was later reported that a civilian, Mr. BUCKLE of Forces Broadcasting Service, had been wounded whilst standing on the verandah of his flat. Order was eventually restored with the cooperation of the Egyptian Police Commandant, using a loud hailer. The body of Major J.C.MCDUALL R.Sigs of GHQ was later found in front of the entrance to the Police Barracks. He had been shot at close range.

2. Throughout Sunday the attitude of the Egyptian police continued to deteriorate and threatening gestures were made towards British troops and vehicles.

In the late afternoon the Egyptian police again began firing indiscriminately at British vehicles and members of the Forces. Police officers appeared to have lost control. Firing continued for some time after dark and BTE advised all British people not on duty to remain in their quarters.

There have been several casualties to both British and Egyptians. It is so far known that British casualties are three officers killed and one seriously wounded, two OR wounded and one Press correspondent wounded. Egyptian casualties as reported to REUTER by the Egyptian Governorate are five police killed and sixteen wounded and three civilians killed and eight wounded.

3. It is most strongly emphasised that when disturbances or firing break out, any person not on duty should remain in quarters or, if on the streets, should immediately take shelter. In no circumstances should individuals take unauthorised part in local military actions or use their firearms except in direct self defence.

4. It is understood that arrangements will be made as quickly as possible to move all families out of ISMAILIA and ARISHIA to safer accommodation.

PORT SAID

5. On 17 Nov an Egyptian threw a can of burning rags into a NAAFI vehicle and during the night 17/18 Nov there were three instances of isolated shots at British guards and patrols.

6. There is evidence of the use by Egyptian thugs of various types of home made bombs and grenades. Two cases were reported during the week-end :-

(a) At 1915 hrs 17 Nov a bomb was thrown by a civilian near the ITV Joury at Ismailia.

(b) at 1920 hrs 17 Nov a bomb was thrown outside the house of Admiral LUCAS of the Suez Canal Company.

Maj G?
Lt Col GS
G (Ops)
19 Nov 51

26. Intelligence summary issued to all units on 19 Nov 51.　　　(D Bowler)

44

CHAPTER THREE

VIOLENCE

During the summer of 1951, tension was rising between the Prime Minister of Egypt, Nahas Pasha, and his people, and he badly needed some political distraction which might bring back his popularity. He chose to resurrect the general desire of his people to rid the country completely of the British presence. Encouraged perhaps by the failure of Britain to prevent the seizure of the Anglo-Iranian Oil Company's installations in Persia by Dr Mossadeq, he decided the time was ripe to try to revoke the Anglo-Egyptian Treaty. As a first step he introduced various provocative measures, including, on 10th August, cancelling authority for the British Army to continue to run main line services over the ESR network. Frantic last minute attempts were made by the West to convert the Canal Zone into a NATO rather than a British base, but these proved fruitless. On 8th October the Egyptian parliament authorised the abolition of the treaty and declared 15th of the month to be celebrated as "Abrogation Day".

The British Army immediately started to put into place emergency measures. The Army and RAF between them employed 66,000 local workers and there was an awareness that they might be inspired by the abrogation celebrations to attack Service personnel and their dependants. Because of this, early in October, married families living in urban areas started being moved into the comparative safety of military compounds. Some of the ugliest scenes on Abrogation Day took place in Ismailia where a crowd of trouble makers from Cairo came in on the morning train, which made an unscheduled stop between Nefisha and Ismailia to allow them to scramble down the embankment. They then attacked Army Mansions, a block of flats occupied by British families in the suburb of Arishia, burned their cars, and then went on to assault and loot the NAAFI shop in Ismailia town centre. There was little effort by the Egyptian police to stop their rampage and order was only restored by the robust actions of the Lancashire Fusiliers.

Similar violence was taking place elsewhere. On 10th October in Suez an RAMC officer's car was set on fire during sporadic outbreaks of rioting, and the situation had deteriorated sufficiently for major precautions to be needed. Sappers serving with 10 Squadron recall the Officer Commanding, Major Alexander, parading the whole unit at 1400hrs in full Battle Order, issuing every man with 20 rounds and sending parties into the town and Port Tewfiq to bring in all the married families.

By 17th October reports were coming in of an Egyptian armoured force advancing along the Cairo to Suez road, and other units were appearing to look equally menacing from the Sinai side of the Canal. The GOC British Troops in Egypt, Lieut General Sir George Erskine, therefore decided to place all his troops on a war footing, and to define a perimeter line round the Zone. Any Egyptian troops crossing this boundary would be regarded as enemy and it became known as the Erskine Line. Across the Suez-Cairo road this line lay at the kilo 99 stone, and the limits of the rail network were defined as Nefisha and Fort Agrud. Responsibility for the operation of the bridge at El Firdan was hotly disputed, until a spirited attack by the British army captured it without casualties to either side.

On Sunday 21st October, as part of the implementation of this plan, 10 Squadron assumed responsibility for the running of the line from Ataka to Fayid. The first stage was to take over all the signal boxes. Escorted by members of the Royal Sussex Regiment, the Sappers rode in on Bren Carriers to the surprise of the natives on duty. Lance Corporal Morgan recalls how he ran up the outside stairs of one box and motioned with his rifle for the Egyptian to move away from the telephones. Fortunately he offered no resistance. However Morgan was a little disconcerted not only to be faced with a seventy lever frame with all the points and signals identified in Arabic, but also because the local employee had his small son with him. Thereafter, as there were not enough men to man all the boxes, it became quite usual for blockmen to travel on the trains, and where necessary walk on ahead to pull off the points, or even for trains to proceed very slowly over them if the points were trailing.

However, this system did not always work out quite as planned. On 16th November, a military freight train had to visit TEK from Suez. On the footplate was Corporal Morgan, who, when the train arrived late that afternoon, walked on ahead up to the signal box to collect the keys to operate the two ground frames, so that the train could cross from the main line into one of the stores sidings. In the middle of this manoeuvre, the train came to a halt. When he went to investigate, it was clear that the engine had jumped the track, leaving its twenty four wagons successfully blocking both the up and down main lines, the siding, and a level crossing. Closer examination showed that some unknown malicious person had half cocked the hand points, and it took a recovery team the whole night to re-rail the loco and reopen the track.

By this time the Egyptian authorities had persuaded the majority of the civilian labour force to abandon their posts en masse, and all available troops were put onto keeping the essential services such as water filtration plants, power stations and lines of communication going. Not only had the main administrative installations been put in jeopardy but all the individuals hitherto employed as unit barbers, domestic staff, cookhouse wallahs, dhobi men, storemen and clerks were being intimidated and many left the camps in which they had been serving. The situation was further aggravated by the formation of a uniformed partisan army of auxiliary police named the Bulak Nazim, specifically to harrass British troops and carry out acts of sabotage.

To relieve the situation the British Government initiated an urgent programme to bring in help from elsewhere. Over the next few weeks some 4000 Mauritian Pioneers arrived. In addition 3000 civilian technicians from Cyprus and Malta, and servicemen from the United Kingdom were brought in, mainly to keep the water, electricity and sewage systems viable. A large number of Reservists were called up in the UK, as part of this programme, including seventy six RE Transportation officers and men of the Special Supplementary Reserve under Lieut Colonel HI Davidson. Among them was Corporal CJ Henry from Blackheath who was already 57 years old and wore 1914-1918 medal ribbons, having left the army in 1921.

It is interesting to note that at one point General Erskine seriously considered cutting off the oil supply to Cairo as it came from Suez. However, he decided that this might provoke retaliation by the Egyptians, who could cut off the Army's only source of fresh water, the Sweetwater Canal.

There was considerable harassment in the Suez area, where on 3rd December, an RE Garrison Engineer captain and several Mauritian soldiers with him were ambushed and killed near a filtration plant. By the following week the situation had become so bad that eighty buildings in the village of Kafr Abdu, which were regularly being used by snipers, were levelled by dozer tanks in Operation Flatten.

On 12th January 1952 a military train approaching TEK was ambushed by armed youths outside the village of El Hammada. The train was brought to a halt, mercifully without casualties. Subsequently a battle ensued when infantry and tanks were called in to drive off the marauders, whose casualties were twelve killed, fifteen wounded and twenty one captured.

As time went on, such attacks became more widespread and ever more vicious, and trains were regularly included in the targets of the terrorists. Three days after the TEK incident, early in the morning, a War Department train heading out from Adabiya was derailed at El Zeitiya outside the oil refinery south west of Suez. As it was probably travelling at about 25 miles an hour when it left the track, the loco "Cpl WJ Lendrim VC", with its tender and seven wagons, came to rest overturned about sixty yards from the point of derailment. The damage

27. The derailed "Cpl Lendrim VC" and wagons outside the Shell Oil Refinery at
El Zeitiya, Suez, after a terrorist attack on the track on 15 Jan 52. Until the
emergency track in the foreground was laid the main supply route from
Adabiya to the rest of the Canal Zone was effectively blocked.

(H Armstrong)

28. The same loco in immaculate livery shortly after her naming ceremony and
before the attack above. *(P Wells)*

29. "C/Sgt Leitch VC" at Kantara January 1952 after a mine had detonated under a driving wheel.
(H Armstrong)

30. Damaged wagons and carriers of the train in the Kantara incident.

(R Thorne)

31. Further damage caused in the Kantara attack   (*A Thorne*)

32. Centurion tanks of 4 RTR on 10 Sqn rail flats at Moascar in Jan 1952 after the Cordon Sanitaire operation.   (*D Bowler*)

33. East African Pioneer
    permanent way working
    parties employed by 10 Rly
    Sqn, at Fanara.
    (D Bowler)

52

to the track, and the base on which it was laid, was so extensive that it was impossible to establish definitely whether fishplates and a length of track had been removed, or whether a mine had been laid. The Egyptian Ministry of the Interior reported that the cause was a mine and that four British servicemen were killed and a sergeant and one other rank wounded. In fact the only casualty mercifully was the flagman on the train who sustained a fractured leg.

Whatever the cause, the disruption was considerable as the line between Adabiya docks and the remainder of the Zone was now completely blocked. The area was swampy and liable to flooding and therefore construction of an alternative track was difficult, but it was imperative that the line was reopened quickly. No breakdown crane was immediately available and so removal of the wreckage was going to be a major problem. The only satisfactory solution was to make use of an adjacent siding clear of the accident and to build an embankment to join it to the main line. Herculean efforts by men of 10 Squadron, the Royal Sussex Regiment and the Royal Pioneer Corps resulted in the new link being virtually completed on the Sunday and the route reopened the next day, six days after the attack.

However this left the problem of removing the wreckage without using the main line for fear of blocking it. By constructing a sleeper roadway first, it was possible to remove the wagons in pieces using a reconditioned mobile crane mounted on caterpillar tracks. As the loco appeared to be in excellent and virtually undamaged condition, despite lying forlornly on its side in the bog, it was decided that an attempt should be made to lift it out bodily. An elaborate recovery operation was then carried out by teams from 10 Squadron, 3 Field Squadron and 53 Port Squadron, involving the construction of overhead lifting gantries. This was not completed until the end of March. Though the wagons were largely cut up and scrapped, the loco was back in service in May.

In January another incident occurred at Kantara, when the loco "C/Sgt P Leitch VC" was mined and its driving wheels blown out. The main frame was so badly damaged that this engine was eventually scrapped. The attack took place on the stretch of line adjacent to the Canal Road, and the loco was heading a composite freight train which included rail flats carrying Bren carriers. Some of the carriers broke loose from their tie-downs when the flats telescoped into each other. Extensive damage was done to both the track and the wagons in this incident, but at least the site was accessible and recovery more straightforward than that at El Zeitya.

Elsewhere, particularly in Ismailia, ugly armed incidents were frequent. Unlike the incident just recorded, some of these were reported in the national press at home, the most serious of which undoubtedly was the attack on a police station which had far reaching repercussions. It arose from the knowledge that much of the persistent harassment was being aided and supported by the police, as a result of which the decision was taken that they should be made to surrender their arms. In some instances they did so with minimum resistance, but at the Bureau Sanitaire, their main headquarters in Ismailia, their response to repeated requests to do so by loud hailer took the form of sustained machinegun fire. Eventually, when it was apparent that further parley was useless, it was decided to use force, and a major attack was launched on 25th January 1952.

By this time 10 Squadron had moved two troops of 4 RTR Centurion tanks on rail flats, headed by "Cpl J Ross VC", from Shallufa to Moascar, and now these tanks were used to fire their main armament at close range into the building, closely followed by infantry clearance parties. By the time the action was over, one hundred and three Egyptians lay dead or wounded, and sixteen British soldiers had been killed. When news of this battle reached Cairo, extensive rioting broke out, and Erskine prepared a major task force to be ready to move to occupy the city to enforce order and protect British nationals. Mercifully this action was not necessary as King Farouk summoned his own troops to clear

34. Christmas card thrown over the wire into Moascar Garrison camp by local
    Egyptians 1952.

(Author)

THE TURNOUTS

By kind permission of Officers Commanding
10th Railway Sqn, R. E. and Married Families Hospital

PRESENTS

The Happiness Express

The Troubadour of Song — L/C. THOMAS

The Inimitable Cox Bros
WITH A SMILE AND A SONG

The Impressionist — Spr. PINSEY

Songs from the Shows Duet
Nurse REED · L/C. THOMAS

The Dithering Doctor — Cpl. THIMARSH
Nurse STONE · Spr. PALMER · Spr. CARROLL

Rhapsody in Blues — Spr. CARROLL
Nurse COLLINS

The Singing Cow Boy — Spr. THOMAS
Nurse STONE · Nurse COLLINS

Three Girls In Harmony — Nurse MILLS
Nurse STONE · Nurse COLLINS

Piano Accordionist — Spr. PALMER

Light Comedy — Spr. JAMMETTS
Spr. SKINNER

Top Three — Spr. SKINNER · Spr. SKINNER

Song With Light Comedy
L/C THOMAS · Spr. COX L. · Spr. COX J. · Spr. PALMER · Spr. SKINNER

Nightingale of Song — Nurse REED

Café in Madrid — Spr. CULLEEN
MOIRA and L/C THOMAS

Song Favourities — Cpl. CULLEEN

The M. E. L. F. Al Jolson — L/Cpl. DAVIES

to be held in the Secondary School Theatre on Friday 28th
March 1952.

Commencing 20.30 Hours.

ADMISSION 10 AND 5 P T.

Andrew's Press. Ismailia

35. 10 Railway Squadron Concert Party programme 1952.

(G V Cox)

56

the streets of rioters, and then summarily dismissed Nahas Pasha for his failure to keep order.

Thereafter, it became common practice to run at least one wagon in front of the locos to reduce the likelihood of major derailments. This precaution proved to be a wise one, as by the end of the emergency there had been no less than twenty eight recorded instances of mines being detonated under trains, including an attempt in May 1952 on "C/ Sgt H McDonald VC".

At Port Said a bizarre and rather happier incident occurred, in complete contrast but typical of the chaotic way of life of those days in the Canal Zone. There was very little accommodation for wives and families and certainly none for those of the massive reinforcements arriving. Indeed many who had been in the theatre for some time had been advised to return home. It was therefore a little incongruous when, blissfully unaware of the warlike footing the Zone was now on, a troopship arrived at Port Fuad whose passengers included a consignment of brides-to-be. They were allowed to disembark, be joined briefly by their fiancees for a marriage service in the chapel, spend a night in Seaview holiday camp, before being re-embarked to return to the United Kingdom the next day!

CHAPTER FOUR

STALEMATE

For the next three years an uneasy period of semi-active service settled on all the units in the Zone, whose strength at its peak rose to 80,000 men. Troops outside camp areas carried arms and all movement by road was carried out under armed escort. Major towns were still out of bounds, and much time and effort was spent providing escorts for soft targets such as NAAFI vehicles and in carrying out basic unit administration and guard duties. Every opportunity was taken by the terrorists to harass the troops and attack them by any means they could. Despatch riders were in danger of being decapitated by trip wires stretched across the roads, so motorcycles were withdrawn. Operational Land Rovers, which usually travelled with their windscreens flat to enable pintle mounted weapons to be used, had a piece of angle iron mounted at the high port on their front bumpers to act as a wire deflector.

Interference with rail communications continued. Typically, early in February 1952, a spike was placed between two rail sections at Fanara causing the wagon in front of the loco to jump the rails, killing the Reservist riding as lookout. Stealing was as widespread as ever, tying down large numbers of troops to protect the many stores dumps and camps. The largest of these, at TEK, was completely surrounded by mines and barbed wire, and covered by searchlights at night, but it was still penetrated regularly by determined thieves. At the southern extremity of the Zone there was a road block manned initially by 10 Squadron (until they moved to Moascar on 10th February 1952), and thereafter by 53 Squadron, controlling all entry into the Canal Zone from the south. They at least had few really ugly incidents, and in fact the early morning duty was often relieved by a friendly challenge to the Sinai Frontier Force, a camel mounted Sudanese unit, returning from patrol.

36. Armoured cars and other vehicles being unloaded onto Z Craft of 1207 Squadron at Port Said 1952.

(D Bowler)

37. Z Craft assembled at Port Said in 1950.

(RE Museum)

38. A group of Egyptians sitting on the bank of the Sweetwater Canal look on as Sappers repair yet another act of sabotage in 1954.

(Author)

39. The LST "Humphrey Gale" tying up at Adabiya 1953.

(Author)

40. 15 cwt truck being loaded as deck cargo by 53 Port Squadron.

(Author)

41. The tanker "World Peace" having collided with the El Firdan bridge January 1955.

(Author)

42. Typical 1950s MT of 53 Port Sqn including Bedford 3 ton and 15 cwt trucks, Austin Pick Up, Standard Vanguard staff car and Matchless 350 cc motor cycles.

(A Trout)

With the rise in strengths of units as a result of the mobilisation of the Supplementary Reserve and the arrival of other reinforcements, some reorganisation became necessary. The Middle East Transportation Regiment units were divided between two commands: Railway Troops Canal Zone (10 Railway Squadron and 169 Railway Workshops) and Port Troops Canal Zone (1207 IWT Squadron and 53 Port Squadron).

Meanwhile, in July, a group of young Egyptian Army officers, led by Colonel Gamel Abdel Nasser, overthrew King Farouk. Brigadier Neguib was promoted to Major General and installed as Prime Minister, and Nasser was made Minister of the Interior. By this time the British Army also had a new GOC, Lieut General Sir Francis Festing, a large man in more senses than one, noted for his ability to travel around the Zone at such speed that he often outstripped his RMP escort vehicles. He was determined that his troops should live as normal a life as the restricted circumstances would allow. Ceremonial parades, for example to honour the Coronation of the Queen in June, were encouraged, and troops began to take part in major training exercises as far afield as the Gebel Ataka and across the Sinai Desert.

However incidents were still occurring which called for firm reprisals. In March 1953 a soldier in Port Said went missing, and was believed to have been abducted. Festing promptly ordered road blocks to be mounted on all communication routes, and all trains stopped and searched. Every signal box in the Zone not already held was duly seized by RE Transportation staff. Trains were stopped repeatedly and the searches carried out very slowly and thoroughly. As the ESR system was still being used by Egyptian civilians from Cairo to meet sailings to and from Port Said, this caused them considerable inconvenience. The action certainly produced the right result, because the missing private reappeared unharmed twenty- four hours later.

Another bizarre incident was the launching in May 1953 of the RE Landship "S.S.Ataqa" by Mrs JC Walkey, wife of the Chief Engineer MELF. Sapper Bob Swarbrick recalls how he and a small team from

53 Port Squadron, under Lt Ellis and WO Phillips, built this steel structure at Adabiya to train recruits in the loading and discharging of seagoing vessels.

In July negotiations began again between the United Kingdom and Egypt concerning the reduction of troops in the Zone. The proposal this time was to establish the Middle East Base in Cyprus rather than Egypt. Little did anyone realise then how short lived such a plan would be as that island was already preparing to seek its own independence from Britain by force within the next two years. In the event, negotiations collapsed when Egypt insisted that, although they were prepared to allow large stocks of stores to remain in the Zone, no uniforms were to be worn by the staff responsible for looking after them.

This condition was not acceptable to the British, and once again tension rose. Armed incidents began to occur more frequently, added to which a total ban on the import of foodstuffs into the Zone was imposed in October. This meant that more stocks had to be imported by sea through military channels such as Adabiya, and infantry and other units regularly had to supply working parties to help unload the stores from lighters. One party on such duty had a narrow escape. Knowing their routine the terrorists had placed a mine, with a time fuse, in a culvert under the road. Fortunately it went off an hour early.

On 17th April 1954 there was a further shift of political power when Nasser became Prime Minister and Neguib took over as President. Initially this did little to alter the level of violence. Shootings and killings continued spasmodically, often by snipers firing at random into camps from outside. Ambushes seldom succeeded, though on one occasion a unit Medical Officer and two other ranks with him were killed in this way. During April and May of this year alone the official weekly Intelligence Reports recorded no fewer than fifty two separate attacks against British Army personnel.

By now the huge panoply of troops and their supporting services had resigned themselves to something of a routine. Over many months every man had become accustomed, not only to the security trials and tribulations, but also to the all pervading smells, including those permanently surrounding the deep trench latrines and the desert rose, and the seemingly endless roar of Hydroburners from the cookhouse. With the typical ingenuity of the British soldier, every effort had been made to make tents more civilised and camps look more attractive. There were now more opportunities to play sport. It was possible latterly for a few wives to join their husbands, and the Parachute Brigade even had the temerity to build their own self-help "Pegasus Village" outside Ismailia.

There being no public transport available to servicemen official recreational transport was provided. 10 Squadron ran trains when necessary to enable men to reach beaches, cinemas and other In-Bound locations. Engrossed in their own activities, the majority of the Army was unimpressed when, in July, agreement was finally reached that civilian contractors would enter the Zone to start to take over and administer the bases the following year. All that concerned them now was the thought that at last they might be going home.

The routines in the docks were changing too. There was an unwritten rule that aircraft carriers homeward bound could carry servicemen's private cars on their decks to the UK for free, on the understanding that if war broke out en route they would be pitched over the side. From time to time therefore such cars were hoisted aboard IWT craft at Fanara and ferried out to the carriers.

These were the years when, perhaps as a result of post-war food shortages in the United Kingdom and the need to avoid waste, the keeping of pigs was a popular pastime. The habit even spread to the military camps in the Zone, despite the fact that 90% of the local population adhered to the faith of Islam and to whom therefore anything to do with the consumption of pork would be forbidden. Enterprising officers, including Major Lynde of 53 Port Squadron, ran highly successful pigsties on the leftovers from the cookhouses. Sapper Mick Reynolds can even recall orders for Pig Wardens being solemnly published, including such instructions as:

"The Pig Warden will be entrusted with the care of the Pigs and will be known as the Prodigal Son and will carry the rank of Swine Major. All casualties, including births, servicing of Lady Pigs, deaths, and the sale of pork will be published in Pig Part 2 Orders."

By October the ban on movement outside the Zone had been lifted, and it was even possible for organised parties to visit Cairo during the day. More normal peacetime ceremonial could be resumed. At a Remembrance Day service in November at St George's Church in Moascar the preacher recalled, how in 1927 when the foundations of the church were being dug, a buried locomotive had been unearthed. This had presumably been dumped in a hole after World War One by troops unable to account for its possession! Events not unlike this were in danger of occurring again. Units all over the Zone, sensing that the end was in sight, were faced with the task of sorting out which stores were to be returned to the UK, which sold, which handed over, and what to do with the inevitable surpluses.

In November 1954, their work done, many of the smaller detachments started to close down. The Fanara Troop of 53 Squadron returned to headquarters, and by January of the following year many members of the unit had been dispersed, either to other squadrons or home depending upon their residual length of service. 53 Squadron itself disbanded in April 1955 and reformed the following month at Longmoor in the UK as 53 Railway Depot Squadron.

Early in January 1955 reports came in to RE Headquarters of the results of another disastrous attempt by a tanker in the Suez Canal to negotiate the bridge at El Firdan. This time it was the 11,000 ton "World Peace" and she did the job thoroughly by bringing about 350 tons of bridge down onto her deck and completely blocking the Canal for four days. Those Sappers present during the repairs could be excused from wondering whether the fact that the accident happened "in the wee sma' hours" of New Years Day had any bearing on the skipper's navigation at the time!

Meanwhile 10 Squadron received a rousing send off from Port Said when they departed in April, and returned to Longmoor in time to celebrate their 150th anniversary. They later became a port squadron and went out to Singapore.

In May the majority of the IWT fleet, including all the remaining Z craft and tugs, being no longer needed in the Canal Zone, were assembled at Port Said in anticipation of their moving to Tobruk, where they were to be mothballed until further notice. This involved some considerable preparation both for the vessels, many of which were not fully seaworthy and therefore unfit to face a long coastal journey, and for the crews. The craft were also used in a frantic effort to get rid of any ammunition that could not be brought home by dumping it in the Mediterranean. It may well be lying on the seabed to this day.

Throughout 1955 the redeployment proceeded apace. The remaining Transportation units were either disbanded or returned to Longmoor and Marchwood in the UK, and by the end of June 1956 the entire military withdrawal was complete.

Within a month, however, political chaos reigned again. On 19th July an Anglo-US financial offer to help Egypt build the Aswan Dam had been withheld and a week later Nasser seized the Canal.

Four months later Allied troops stormed Port Said and British troops were back on Egyptian soil. But that is another story.

POSTSCRIPT

Action in the Canal Zone over these years was in many ways a bewildering experience for the soldier in the British Army. Having only recently won a war that was quite clearly a war, with a recognisable distinction between enemy and friendly troops, this was something different. It was, in fact, an early example of the type of Internal Security emergency with which the Army was to become only too familiar in later years in Malaya, Kenya, Cyprus, the Far East, the Radfan, and eventually in Northern Ireland. What made matters worse was that it had to be carried out in such a hot, unpleasant, unhealthy and fly-ridden place.

Moreover, far from being a full-blown confrontation between Great Britain and Egypt, there was at no time any breakdown in diplomatic relations between the two countries, even at the height of the riots. Numbers of British ex-patriots who were living in Cairo and Alexandria appear to have remained largely oblivious to what was going on elsewhere, preoccupied with continuing the social round they had resumed after the end of the War. The Ambassador, for example, continued to hold a duck shoot in the Delta not far from TEK, in which British troops were asked to help, even during the troubles. One section of the Army, the RAMC Malaria Control Unit, bearing a white flag with this insect prominently displayed on its Land Rovers, continued to operate in hostile villages with impunity throughout this period.

Today, few people have any contact with members of the Armed Services. This was not the case in the 1950s, when the army was over three times the size it is today, and included a large number of National Servicemen. There were, as a result, many more wives, families and friends at home in the UK, directly concerned with the welfare of those serving in the Canal Zone. Family morale was not improved when it became known, as it did quite frequently, that their loved ones were being kept on beyond their original dates for release "because of the State of Emergency". The precise details of this "Emergency" kept altering: some weeks were designated as being "on Active Service" and some not, with significant effect, for example, on the punishments which could or could not be awarded by military courts.

Probably what rankled most, and still does to the survivors today, is that no General Service Medal was awarded, even to those involved in operations at the end of 1951 and beginning of 1952. Over the five months between 17th October and 21st March fifty-four British servicemen were killed and at least sixty-nine wounded. Thus many more were killed in the Canal Zone than in the emergencies in Kenya (12) and Borneo (16). For service in each of these theatres a campaign medal was awarded. General Sir Brian Robertson, as C-in-C MELF, made representations to the War Office in January 1952, but the case was rejected by the Army Council. General Erskine is alleged to have had to explain to his men that "the Foreign Office did not want to offend the Egyptians". This did not stop the latter awarding a medal to those members of their police and paramilitary forces who took part. Various efforts have been made by Members of Parliament over the years to have this omission corrected but so far without success, and there the matter rests today.

ANNEX A

Stanier 8F 2-8-0 Locomotives serving in the Middle East and named after RE Crimean War holders of the VC

Number	Nameplate	Remarks
70320	Lt WO Lennox VC	Returned to UK. Scrapped 1965
70373	C/Sgt H McDonald VC	Transferred to ESR
70387	Cpl WJ Lendrim VC	Ditto
70395	Capt HC Elphinstone VC	Ditto
70501	Spr John Perie VC	Ditto
70516	Cpl J Ross VC	Ditto
70574	C/Sgt P Leitch VC	Scrapped Suez 1954
70575	Sgt J Smith VC	Returned to UK Scrapped 1959
70593	Lt G Graham VC	Transferred to ESR

A small plaque was fitted in each cab carrying an engraving of the citation.

Some of the original nameplates are now in the RE Museum at Chatham.

(Source: MOD Handbook)

Transportation Chain of Command Oct 1951

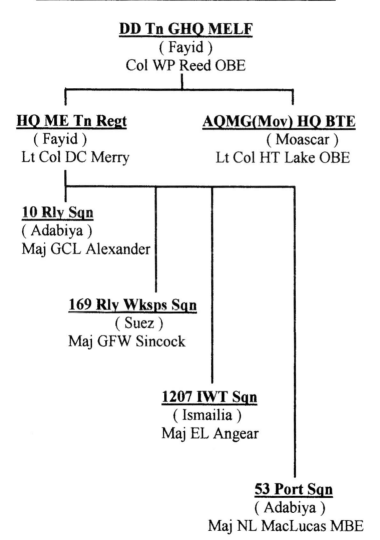

DD Tn GHQ MELF
(Fayid)
Col WP Reed OBE

HQ ME Tn Regt
(Fayid)
Lt Col DC Merry

AQMG(Mov) HQ BTE
(Moascar)
Lt Col HT Lake OBE

10 Rly Sqn
(Adabiya)
Maj GCL Alexander

169 Rly Wksps Sqn
(Suez)
Maj GFW Sincock

1207 IWT Sqn
(Ismailia)
Maj EL Angear

53 Port Sqn
(Adabiya)
Maj NL MacLucas MBE

Acknowledgements

My thanks are due to the Directorate of Military Survey for providing contemporary maps from their archives. Much of the background historical material has been taken from Blaxland's "The Regiments Depart" and I have also drawn freely from "Soldier" magazine and articles that have appeared in the Royal Engineers Journal.

Above all I am indebted to many veterans of the period for much of the material on which this book is based. I have received so many anecdotes, photographs and memorabilia concerning their time in the Middle East that it has simply not been possible to include more than a fraction. In particular I would like to thank the following for their contributions:

Hugh Armstrong.	Ray Howells
Ken Arrowsmith.	Ross Mason
Leonard Ball.	Doug Morgan
Ramon Blake.	John Morgan
David Bowler.	Mick Reynolds
John Bowman.	Malcolm Rhodes
Peter Broxham.	Ivan Rickwood
Jack Clarke.	Frank Sutton
David Cobbett.	Bob Swarbrick
Geoff Cox.	Robin Thorne
Bob Crane.	Danny Tongs
Stewart Currie.	Alan Trout
Roy Ellis.	David Waller
Victor Garratt.	George Walters
George Harris.	Wally Warren
Michael Henry.	David Webber
David Hickman.	Phil Wells